Trillions & Trillions of Heartbeats

Illustrations by Ted Keller
Layout and Design by Howard Kirk Besserman

Also by Meg Hamill

Death Notices
(Factory School Press, 2007)

Resonant Books
P.O. Box 4474
Santa Rosa, CA 95402

ISBN: 978-0-9816714-0-6

Printed by AngelPrint
on paper that is 100% Recycled and
100% Post-Consumer Waste

Trillions & Trillions of Heartbeats

by Meg Hamill
Illustrated by Ted Keller

Resonant Books, 2008

Acknowledgments

Thank you to Jess Perlitz for providing the image of the Lake Pedder Earthworm, and the grass. Thank you to Nick for listening to these poems as they were taking shape. Thank you to all that had to happen in order for you, dear reader, to be holding this book in your hands right now. Thank you to all the people, and the money, and everything the people did to get the money, to the trees and the earth, to the recycling plant, to the clean water and the critters, to the wind turbines and the wind...Thank you.

Contents

Introduction

Everything that is happening to us, all the catastrophes and the miracles, all the wars and gardens blooming, the extinctions and the nests full of eggs, are contained within one lush sphere that is spinning and hovering, amid trillions of other spheres, and exploding stars, and expanding mushroom clouds of gas, all suspended together in an unimaginable stillness and darkness. When I zoom out like this, I get the overwhelming sense that all is well, that the seriousness with which we examine our lives, individually and collectively, is strangely out of proportion.

And then I zoom in. I watch the presidential debates on TV. I read books about genetically modified foods. I watch the weather patterns changing. I read about the depleted oceans and the plight of the honeybee. I hear people saying as goes China, so goes the planet, and other people talking about how the current environmental crisis is probably the greatest challenge that humanity has ever faced.

We are seeing more clearly than ever before, how our daily actions affect the air and the water and the earth, the neighboring towns, states, and countries, other cultures and ways of life. When I zoom in, it's so easy to see how each action and each decision is indeed laden with importance. From this perspective, what is at stake, personally and globally, politically and spiritually, seems unfathomably significant.

In this book I recorded 23 animals that have recently disappeared from the planet due to human-induced causes. This subject matter was tricky to maneuver. Whenever the writing began to bend towards a call to action, or towards that subtle desire to change someone's way of thinking, or whenever it simply began to indulge in itself, I would feel in my body an unmistakable sensation that I was heading in the wrong direction. It felt like I was clenching my fist around the idea that things should be somehow different than they are. As I navigated towards a way of writing that felt more authentic, the fist only began to unclench when I could drop the filters of "good," "bad," "should," and "shouldn't," and allow all that is happening to live simply within these poems, unclouded by my own guilt, fear, blame or judgment.

These poems take the form of laments. They are written from the perspective that all is unimaginably well, and they are written simultaneously from the perspective that all is not at all well. To me, both of these ways of seeing feel equally true.

Banded Rail of Chatham Island
or Moeriki

Rallus dieffenbachii

Moeriki this winter I sat in cafes. I made space around my self. I thought about what it means to be dead and what it means to be alive. In the cafes there was lots of coffee to drink and all the beings drinking the coffee appeared to be alive.

Sometimes they had a brightness in their eyes which I took to mean that those particular ones were very much alive.

Moeriki you came out from the reeds at dusk and dawn. You came out with a brightness in your eyes. You came out when you could hide in heavy rains. Moeriki you came out in the gloaming in the heavy rains to wade in wetlands to bring food back to your nests where there were babies vulnerably squawking for you.

In the graveyards of my species Moeriki there are rows and rows of white stones. All the white stones are the same height and width and the graveyard looks like math looks when it is very simple.

Moeriki you fed on beetles and crabs, spiders and worms. You had a slim body to navigate through the reeds and a short tail that flicked up and down as you walked.

Moeriki on the other side do we get so easily confused? Do we get so easily derailed? On the other side is it really any different than being alive? I have the intuition that it is not really different. I have the intuition that it will move quick, but it will be just as easy to get our tires stuck in the mud for a very long time.

Moeriki of Chatham Island, 370 miles east of New Zealand where you once built your fragile nests in the tall reeds on the ground, there is a silent ringing space. There is a strange cavity. There is an invisible, gaping hole where we lost you. Moeriki this strange cavity, this ringing hole, doesn't answer any of my questions and in this answerless place there are no neat rows. There are no garlands of flowers. There are no mathematical explanations.

Moeriki the rats and the cats that we introduced to your island found your babies squawking in fragile nests. When we lit fires in the bushes and in the reeds to clear the

land for farms, the fires licked and swallowed your feathers and your babies squawking in fragile nests.

Moeriki there is a lush and spherical web. I know that the spherical web is a network of knots and threads that spreads like a blanket stitching us to it over the geography of wherever we happen to be living, and I know the web keeps going beyond the horizon to where everything else is living, the same network of knots and threads slipping over the rim of the Pacific, stitching us to itself with absolute grace, mercilessly.

We have never not been all sewed in, even the gaping hole, the silent cavity, the ringing place where we lost you Moeriki just gets sewn right back in.

Tecopa Pupfish

Cyprinodon nevadensis calidae

Tecopa, Tecopa, you were barely as long as a toenail Tecopa. Tecopa you made your home in the little salty pools and thermal springs near Death Valley Tecopa. Tecopa I make my home on Clarke Street in apartment number two. Tecopa I sleep in a big bed that cost a thousand dollars with a pile of books all open to the first page.

Tecopa you thrived in waters up to 108 degrees Fahrenheit. Tecopa I thrive in Oakland on Clarke Street next to Carl's Juniors and the Macarthur Bart and I have the sounds of the freeway always here with me. Sometimes in the morning I pretend the freeway is a forest of Douglas-firs with the wind blowing through them, because it does sound like a gentle wind through the firs. The freeway is that constant. It is that enveloping us all the time here on Clarke Street Tecopa.

Tecopa what does it mean to have lost you? You who produced two to ten generations in a year, you who fed off the blue-green algae from the hot spring, Tecopa, just as we started to know you, just as we started to know you. Tecopa when those little salty pools and thermal springs where you made your home were channeled in the 1940's by the builders of a bathhouse, suddenly the waters were too swift for you. Tecopa how does one know when the waters are too swift for you? How do we know when we can't adapt any more to how swift the waters are and instead of adapting just break open our hearts and die?

And then the mosquito fish were introduced Tecopa who liked the taste of you. The last of you was spotted in the 1970's in an artificial pond and creek at Jed's Motel in Tecopa Hot Springs. Tecopa the bathhouse has long since gone bankrupt and been deserted.

Tecopa how is it being dead? I am practicing dying each moment when my body exhales its inspiration. Tecopa I am practicing how death is the same as being alive and I am getting confused about which part is dying and which part is living. Death brings such an opportunity Tecopa, such an opportunity to break open our hearts. Tecopa the waters are getting swift here too Tecopa. In Oakland they are getting there. I'm wondering when they will get too swift for me and when I will stop being able to adapt to them Tecopa, and instead wake up and break open my heart and die with each exhalation all day.

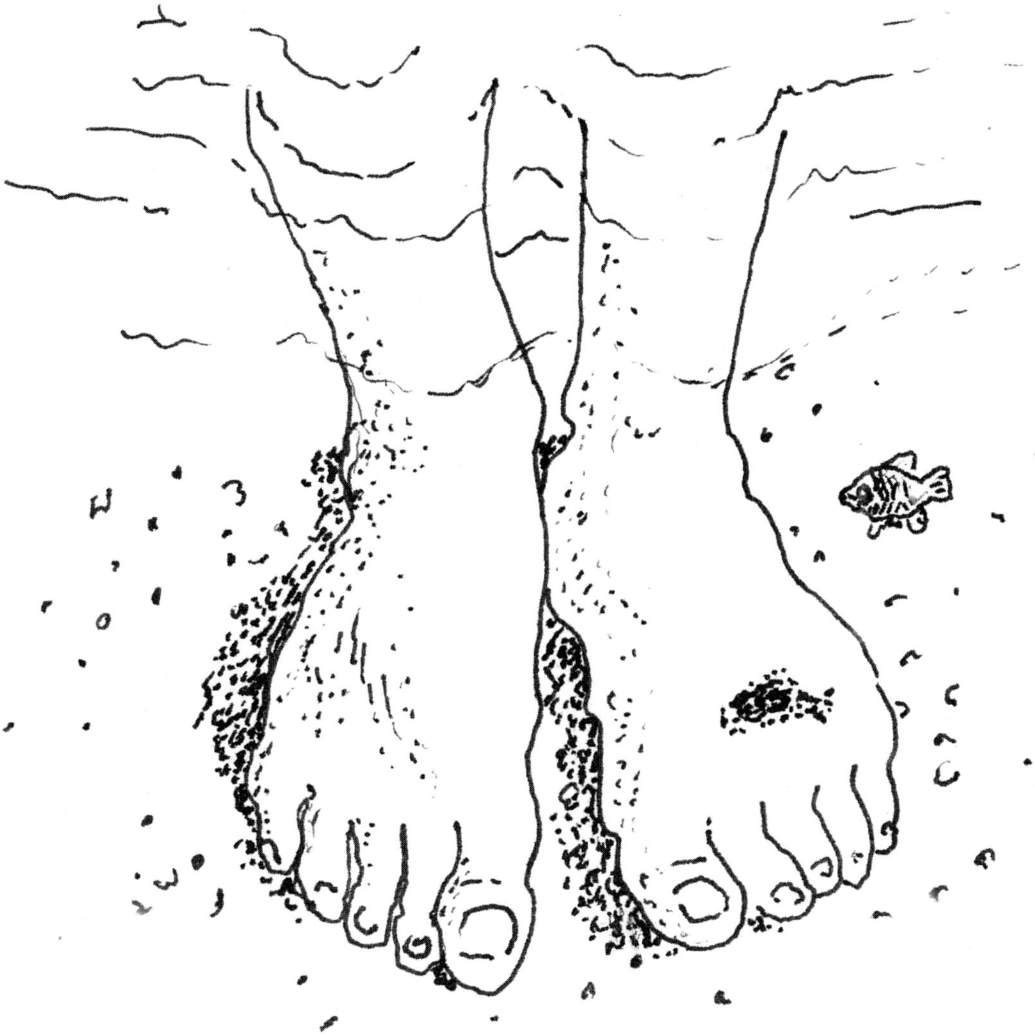

Bubal Hartebeest

Alcelaphus buselaphus buselaphus

Bubal I have learned all the words for things. I have learned the words for countries and flowers and automobiles and all the different types of clouds, words for neurotic tendencies and obsessive thought patterns and all the Buddhas and Bodhisattvas throughout space and time.

They say the moment you teach a child the name bird, the child never sees the bird again. Hartebeest is an Afrikaans word that means tough beast.

Bubal I'm helpless to all these words. I'm down on my knees this morning and holding up my arms to try to get one real breath in between this incessant wording of things.

Bubal you were once the widest ranging antelope in Africa. Bubal you were entirely pale reddish yellow except for the long hairs at your tail. Bubal even your irises were yellow.

Bubal I am up early with the garbage trucks working on a new worldview. I am jetlagged and the quails are calling. Bubal I am down on my knees this morning and holding up my arms.

Bubal of characteristic lyre-shaped horns, Bubal of large herds in the mountains of Algeria, Bubal domesticated by ancient Egyptians and used as a sacrament, Bubal hunted out by French colonels in large massacres of game.

Bubal from you I learn how it does and it doesn't seem to matter that much when things disappear, how it does and at the same time how it does not affect much of anything to be holding a fist above a head, amid thousands of fists held up high above thousands and thousands of heads, how it doesn't seem to matter that much that your name meant tough beast in Afrikaans.

Bubal you were one name sprung from the nameless. You were one form sprung from the formless, and to the formless there is a way of speaking that does not happen in names. Bubal you have been recycled into all the bodies in all the African towns that are toiling now and resting now and toiling now and resting now. I am holding up my arms Bubal and I am down on my knees, trying to see you clearly for a moment, trying to see you in that very clear space where we see ourselves lighted up in everybody else.

Palestinian Painted Frog
or Israel Painted Frog

Discoglossus nigriventer

This afternoon the sun is out and it is doing like an aperture to all the cells and to the organs of all the people on all the outdoor benches, to all the people sitting on stoops.

Today my cells just ate a Tuscan crepe and are greeting French Roast that is very dark and a little bit too strong.

Palestinian Israel Painted Frog with a dark belly and small white spots, you are gone from the world and your absence is a price that we have paid for being exactly how we are.

Palestinian Israel Painted Frog, ochre above and olive-grey beneath, known only from the Eastern shores of the Hula Wetlands in Northern Israel. Frog your wetland was torn apart by people believing strongly in things, by people taking positions on certain political or developmental things. Frog your posthumous name change by the Israeli government has been referred to as another attempt by Zionists to erase any vestige of the name "Palestine" from human memory. And now frog you are becoming a symbol. Your name pops up in pro-Palestine arguments all over the world.

Frog I believe strongly in things too. There are places that get torn apart because I hold on with a very tight fist to these beliefs. Perhaps not wetlands get torn apart, perhaps it is the space between myself and another human being that gets torn apart, but I can see very clearly how it is not different, all these ways we tear our Self apart.

Tasmanian Wolf
or Thylacine

Thylacinus cynocephalus

Thylacine you were a marsupial. You were a dog in the deserts of Tasmania with a pouch in your belly just like a kangaroo. Thylacine when your babies were too big for the pouch they still tried to climb back in. Thylacine you learned from the kangaroo and you learned from the wolf and you took what was good from both of them and over many lifetimes you became yourself.

Thylacine, marsupial, pouched desert dog, what is this clouded veil through which the world appears? This veil that keeps us very busy with ourselves, that keeps us spinning around the racetrack of our self, this veil that can only be named veil because I have seen it lift up to reveal a place where everything is shimmering.

Thylacine in the 19th century bounty hunters were paid 25 cents a scalp for you, in a concerted effort to eradicate you entirely from the continent, and today the Australian conservation foundation offers 100 dollars just for a sighting of your tracks but so far there have been none.

Thylacine I don't know what we can learn from you. I don't know what can we take from you that is good, and over this very lifetime use this knowledge to become more fully ourselves. Thylacine we are nobodies holding on to other nobodies in warm, soft beds, in cold, desert dens. We are gifted with a way of seeing, and through this way of seeing the world appears. We are gifted with these laps upon laps that we run around our self, these laps so glaringly repetitive that they lead us inevitably to our Self.

Kusai Island Crake

Aphanolimnas monasa

Thank you to all that is. Thank you for all the birds and thank you for taking them away.

If I can look beyond this land that this home is on, beyond this ridge, beyond the water table 128 feet below what it was before, beyond the cows with yellow numbers punched in their ears, beyond the fields with the spider webs swinging, beyond the neighbors with their deep grooves. If I can look as far out as I can to where the world is spinning around, to where neglect gives off a certain hue, before body language or words are given.

If I can say thank you again and again, thank you for the time of the big mammals and thank you for the time of taking them away. Thank you for the time of infrastructure powered by oil and thank you for the time of taking all the oil away.

Amid the offshore winds, amid the soft breeze that is blowing from the East but soon will be blowing from the West, amid the early morning in the air that smells like burning houses, amid the piles of papers and the attention to detail it takes to be a part of this world,

amid the seasons turning, amid the gardens blooming and the guns shooting, the Kusai Island crake disappeared from the world, the nearly flightless island coastal swamp insectivore, the somewhat chicken-shaped bird with rounded wings, a short tail, large feet and long toes.

The crake that in the olden days had been a sacred bird, until the Christian missionaries came and people stopped paying attention to the older faiths, the crake that was eaten by rats washed ashore from a shipwreck.

Thank you for the crake and for the rats. Thank you for the time of the older faiths and thank you for the time of taking the older faiths away.

To simply wait and watch the world as it is changing, and wait and wait for whatever is happening and whatever is going to happen.

While we are waiting this bird can become a container for us. It can become a way of looking at what is happening while it is happening, to get the feel of this extinction while it is underway instead of waiting until later, without judgment, without knowing which species should survive and which species should disappear, without blaming anyone, without blaming ourselves.

It can become a way of seeing what is happening through a veneer of feathers that are really just full of empty space, while we are breathing in the smoke from fires burning all over California today.

Marbled Toadlet

Uperoleia marmorata

This is not a special story. There is so little to say that it is barely a story. The Toadlet lived in Australia and is now preserved in formaldehyde in a jar. There is no other evidence or specific feeding habits or mating calls recorded. There are no colors recorded or data regarding how the colors differed from male to female. In the jar the toad's lips are pointing up and he is the color of hay.

How do we know we are changing as we are changing or is it only in retrospect that how we changed becomes clear? How do we know we are not changing as we are not changing? How does the feeling of being stagnant feel different as it is happening than the feeling of movement?

Listen to the rain in that moment when it finally arrives at the earth. Listen to the violence today all over the world. Listen to the toadlet taking up space and to the subtle noises of non-existence. Listen to the airplanes going by and afterwards to the dead grasses getting blown.

Every moment seems to give itself to the next without any wrenching or holding on.

Listen to this cow with a yellow number punched in her ear walking uphill with full udders. Listen to the glaciers all over the world abandoning themselves to clear blue rivers and streams. Look up at the sky and the strata of clouds in the sky and try to get the feel of it just as it is passing overhead.

Alien Splitfin

Chapalichthys peraticus

Here is where we all are, the bones and the dreams and the documents and illustrations of us all, the breath and heartbeats and still sleeping parts of us all, sailing around and around on this magnificent, spherical ship, hovering all together in an unimaginable vastness. So together here that it is difficult to comprehend just how together, so demandingly are we set down here on this spinning sphere together, that it seems much easier to believe in a dream called there is no such thing as together. Splitfin the different decades, the different freezes and thaws, the different disasters are like costumes that we wear.

Alien splitfin, 16.5 million years ago your ancestors were twirling in the shallow fresh waters of the mesas just west of Mexico City, learning how to procreate, how to swim efficiently and quickly, how to know what parts of themselves to build up and what parts to let go.

Splitfin 11 million years before humans split off from other apes your family was paddling around there in schools, evolving into subspecies there in the sweet, dangerous waters full of silt and sand.

And splitfin here we all still are, you lodged in the fossil records, you dead bone lodged in the sand, me with a heartbeat taking trips in airplanes, me holding babies in my arms, me being stripped of all the subtle ways that I keep myself separate from everybody else. We are twirling around and around, all together on this exquisite boat, hovering all together in this startling vastness. The different decades, the different shapes of our forms, the different disasters are like costumes that we wear.

Przewalski's Horse
or Wild Horse

Equus caballus

Przewalski's horse you are stockier than domesticated horses. You have shorter legs that are faintly striped. Your dark brown mane stands erect.

Wild horse you travel in herds three to six miles in a day within a well-defined home range, sleeping for four hours at night. Horse your herds include a dominant stallion, a dominant mare, other mares and your offspring.

Wild horse I am breaking apart a small bubble made of the things I have been taught to make my life out of, a bubble inside of which I hoped that I was safe, but I don't know if I want to be safe like that anymore. Inside the bubble it was usually warm enough and there was enough food to eat. Inside of it I had birthdays and different jobs and the seasons spun around and around.

Wild horse, in breaking apart this bubble there are glimpses of myself embedded in a larger, softer self. In the larger softer self there is ventilation. There are still all the neurotic tendencies and all the seasons spinning and sometimes it is difficult to sleep. There are still the jobs and the different houses. But suddenly also there is the world blowing through, with all of its heartache and its fear and its bullets embedding into itself, with its love and gentle arms that wrap around itself. There is the war blowing through and there is the extinction blowing through. There are orchards drooping with fruit blowing through. There is the jungle blowing through. There are big changes blowing through. Not getting lodged inside but blowing all the way through.

Horse your ancestors have been hunted for a thousand years.

Horse by the beginning of the 20th century all the wild ones among you were confined to Mongolia and adjacent parts of China, and then by the 1970's there were nearly no more wild ones among you, and though some of the wild ones among you have bred with domestic ones and there is a reintroduction program in Poland to reintroduce the domesticated wild ones among you back into the wild, all the really wild ones among you are gone.

Horse life continues in the same way it was continuing before as long as I imagine it to be the same way that it was. Horse somewhere in the world you are learning to be wild again. Today the wind is blowing in fresh air from the coast and blowing in traffic sounds from the Bohemian Highway, today as the sun is shining and the vultures have just found a fresh meal. Horse today the outside of the bubble mirrors the inside of the bubble but only exactly so.

White-Fin Dolphin
or Baiji or Goddess of the River*

Lipotes vexillifer

Happy New Year said the country band as we were swinging around and around, as the women in high heels were jiggling their hips and swinging around. Happy New Year the country band said as we were honking our party horns.

Today it is the New Year and it is warmer than it should be. Start building your underground house said Carol when I brought her the rent check. Happy New Year she said as Chloe the dog was barking, as the sun was shining, as she handed me a big bag full of truffles.

For 20 million new years the White-Fin Dolphin or Baiji swam China's longest river, the Yangtze, but a recent expedition failed to spot a single one and conservationists fear the almost-blind, long-beaked animal is the first big, aquatic mammal to become extinct due to human activity.

It used to be worshipped as a goddess by the Chinese. According to legend the Baiji is the reincarnation of a princess who refused to marry a man she did not love, and was drowned by her father for shaming the family.

Dolphin, Baiji, White-Fin Goddess of the River, I am going to focus my attention on you. I am not going to flinch for awhile or wish you back again dolphin. While I am praying for you dolphin help me to create a new way of looking, so that through looking we may begin to register these things differently, to register what is happening with more clarity and with less of the filter called everything-we-have-already-seen and the other filter called everything-we-know-to-be-true.

* One Baiji was possibly sighted August 19th, 2007 in the Yangtze River close to Tongling City in Anhui Province. A man saw a white object swimming in the river and filmed it. No one could confirm the sighting, as the video was of very poor quality and taken from about 1,000 meters away.

Sumatran Rabbit

Nesolagus netscheri

I dreamed of leading children down city streets away from a war. I dreamed a bobcat came to our house with a message that didn't happen in words and then I dreamed about a city that had ghosts in it leftover from a war.

There is a gap that is trying to cave in upon itself, that is fruitlessly, endlessly, through all the states of anxiety, trying to become filled with something less terrifying than itself. As if there could be something layered upon the gap that was not at its most essential nature made from the same empty space, or as if empty space had cracks through which it could possibly get filled with something other than itself. Before it tries though, it is luminous the gap, and in the trying it is also luminous. And in the aftermath it is luminous still.

My friends, we are treading water on top of an ocean so deep and so dazzlingly dark, that to plunge down at all is to grapple with the possibility that there is no return to where the water is warmer, to where there are lifeboats, and goals to swim towards.

In the gap there is no such thing as a disaster. The different disasters, the different decades are like costumes that the world will wear.

This morning there is a small rabbit, whose disappearance, for all intents and purposes, appears to be disastrous, pushing in against the gap, a rabbit with short ears and soft fur and a bright red rump and tail, the rabbit who came out only at night in forested altitudes of the Barisan range of mountains in Southwest Sumatra, where forest clearance has destroyed much of the habitat, the rabbit last sighted in 1978 though that last sighting couldn't even be for sure.

Dear rabbit, the destruction continues in your home range at an average rate of 4.85 kilometers squared per month.

Rabbit, let me hold you close to my heart as I live my life today, in a world so filled with paradox, that I can actually go about believing that I belong only to myself. Dear rabbit, the way I hold you close, the way that I forget to hold you close, the way I see the world as a miracle and then it is, the way I see the world with a certain blandness, and immediately, so it is.

Lovegrass Noctuid Moth

Hypena plagiota

Lovegrass Noctuid Moth that is the most beautiful name I've ever heard, Lovegrass that grows in bunches with a weeping habit, Lovegrass densely tufted in Africa, fed to cattle as fodder and sometimes to humans in a famine, Lovegrass whose seeds latch on to the passing animals with hooks, Lovegrass Noctuid Moth listed as extinct in 1996, Lovegrass a name followed by a Latin name in a long list of names without any details following them.

It is the driest January on record Lovegrass Noctuid Moth and again today the skies are clear and blue, again today on the corner of Third Street and E Street there is a man waving a rainbow flag as big as a swimming pool that says PEACE, all by himself there on the corner, waving his flag. We are all working in the ways that we know how Noctuid Lovegrass, in the ways that we've been taught, and then later on after we've exhausted all the ways that we've been taught, we keep working in the new ways that we are making up for ourselves.

Lovegrass Noctuid Moth invariably attracted to light, when I realized Lovegrass that there was no path, when I went to work and the path to follow became like a mirage, when I was always falling off the path Lovegrass even if I could feel with my feet that people had gone there before, like there were footprints to put my footprints inside of and yet I kept falling off somehow even though the footprints were there.

Lovegrass Noctuid robustly built moth, flying around the islands at night, Lovegrass with your drabness and your eggs in the dirt, with your larvae that fed at night, hiding in a crevice of their food plant during the day, larvae that formed a hard shiny pupae. Lovegrass Noctuid this is only noise but it is some noise for you. This is only noise filled with cracks in the noise, filled with doubt and shame and love and all the things that I feel today upon waking, and yet Lovegrass it is a gift for you, for you who found the other side of all this drought and all this flag-waving, for you who found the other side of all this noise.

Ivell's Sea Anemone

Edwardsia ivelli

Fluttering flower of shallow mud bottoms, transparent hero of long hovels, lolling in the soft mud bottoms of the lagoon. Ivell's sea anemone classified as data deficient on the IUCN Red List in 2004, anemone known only from the Widewater Lagoon in West Sussex, England, anemone first discovered in 1975 and last recorded in 1983, anemone an eight-year span when we found you nestling in the soft mud of the lagoon, and then for 24 years we haven't found you since, you simple animal made up of a column with a mouth and twelve transparent tentacles, you buff colored with orange spots, you tentacles spotted with brown and cream.

But this is not about the anemone, not really. It is not about the passing of forms or the temperatures rising. it is not about mourning or paying homage to the forms or going to the empty space that once held all the forms. It is not about the IUCN Red List of threatened species with all of its taxonomy and detailed documentation. It is not so much about the news each day, or the seasons passing, or the fate of the planet, or whether or not we can work hard enough and fast enough to save ourselves from destroying ourselves.

The nature of everything is to become something else, and like everything is in its own way, this project is a document of everything becoming something else.

Sea Mink

Mustela macradon

Maine of red Yugo, Maine of big wheels, Maine of gardens of kale green through the winter, Maine of long table with china on it, with a turkey dinner on it, Maine the feeling moves quickly to behind the eyes, and in the feeling is the feeling of all the eyes around the table looking into all the other eyes around the table, or else dodging all the eyes around the table for years, and in the dodging, and in the gazing into is born a web built of millions of very, very strong threads.

Maine of Yugo I push, Maine of islands and shacks on the islands, and seals following us in our rickety boat out to the islands, Maine of thick accent and a muck-bottom lake.

Maine of the Sea Mink that disappeared 80 years before I was born, Sea Mink bigger than a fox, though not much, who took refuge in holes or cracks of the ledges, who were dislodged by men working with shovels and crow bars, Sea Mink who were caught by dogs when they came out.

Maine of rugged coastline and rolling hills, Maine that has popping the cherry and LSD sewn into the threads, that has a German girl and years of meals at a long table spun into the threads, Maine of parties in gravel pits and bonfires fueled by tires, Maine of parents who are sick of Maine, who have their prayer flags flapping in the below zero wind chills of Maine, praying get me out Maine, all spun into the very strong threads.

Maine of snowmobiles and loons, Maine of the Sea Mink over hunted for furs, who were shot and pulled out by means of an iron rod with a screw at the end or repeated firings of pepper into the hole, Mink who survived somehow the frozen winter oceans of the rugged coast of Maine until the price of furs reached 10 dollars.

Maine of leaf peepers, Maine of cone eaters, Maine of strong threads, Maine of taking the very strong threads in my hand like a weaver and deciding what to do with them, deciding what kind of pattern, at least in the moments when there appears to be a choice.

Lake Pedder Earthworm

Hypolimnus pedderensis

I am researching the Lake Pedder earthworm, only known by a specimen collected from a beach on Lake Pedder in Tasmania in 1971, Lake Pedder that was a jewel in the wilderness, a magnificent untouched natural formation, Pedder that instilled wonder in all who had the good fortune to visit. I am sitting in a cafe in a very small town watching the landscape flood. It is the middle of February and I am new to this town.

Earthworm you had only one home. You never found a new home. You weren't as adept as we are at breaking out of the limitations of ecosystems. And in this way you filled a niche and did not cause much destruction. You did not travel long distances to seek a better life for your children. You stayed on the beach and dug holes in the sand, and then we came to the beach with our big-tired machines, with our deep-seated instinct to make our lives more comfortable for ourselves.

Earthworm in 1972, your Lake Pedder was inundated for hydroelectric power generation and three dams now exist on the impoundment. Earthworm a survey in 1996 was carried out to determine the conservation and taxonomic status of you, and to determine whether or not you still existed. Directed sampling of the area leading to the original collection site failed to find you worm, and thus you are considered likely to be extinct due to inundation of your original and unique habitat.

Earthworm, we are simple spaces covered in skin where there is life happening. We are patches of awareness, amid trillions and trillions of patches of awareness. We are creatures in the end. We are creatures just like you were a creature and peacocks are. We are creatures of habit and creatures with terrifying stories of courage and abuse. Worm we are creatures beautifully adapted to find what is beautiful in each moment. We are creatures like rhinos and elephants, with their glorious tusks and their armor and their horns. We are just as impeccably designed and just as flawed. We are just as hardwired with the instinct to survive. Earthworm we are so together here it is difficult to fathom how together we are.

Cascade Funnelweb Spider

Hadronyche pulvinator

Spider sometimes I wonder if I will always remain out here at the shore of my illusion, where it is sandy and nothing envelops me totally and completely, where there are fireworks and different newspapers to read, and an infinite number of spaces to get stuck. And then I wonder spider if there is anywhere to stay in the shallow places of the illusion, because really it seems spider like all the shallow parts are leading to the deep parts eventually, and the deep parts are leading to where there is no illusion anymore, which is where you have gone spider, as far as my rational mind can tell, and which is where I am going too spider, eventually, as far as my rational mind can tell.

Inside the bigger illusion recently somewhere quietly and very far from here spider, you came and went from the tangled web of illusion, without many fireworks or newspaper columns speaking out or fighting for the protection of, or gathering precious footage of you.

You Cascade funnelweb spider, first described by Hickman in 1926 when he found two of your burrows in soft soil near the bank of a creek. One burrow was about 18 centimeters deep with a silk tube inside. He sketched the burrow, an egg capsule, and your eyes.

Cascade funnelweb, one to five centimeters in size, with a glossy carapace, long spinnerets and fangs that pointed straight down and did not cross each other, spider with ample venom glands. Spider you could move very quickly across the ground and were unable to climb well because of your bodyweight. Spider you lunged for your prey using venom and pincers.

Spider there have been no sightings or records of you for over 50 years and the place where you were found has now been destroyed through suburban growth.

Spider was it full of anguish inside of your tiny being, when you were down to the dregs of your species? Was it like a dream when you were down to the last scattered few? Was it confusing to not find any one, no matter how long you walked, no matter how many webs you spun? Were you searching and searching until the end? Was it full of a sinking, desperate feeling, or was it actually lovely to feel that free?

Llin Island Cloud Rat

Crateromys paulus

Llin Island cloud rat, nocturnal forest rodent of the Philippines, arboreal slow moving herbivore, preyed upon by very large birds, Llin Island cloud rat hunted by Filipinos for food, cloud rat of course fur, of bushy tail, cloud rat resembling a large squirrel, crepuscular Llin Island cloud rat who the locals refer to as Yut Yut.

Here we go again Llin Island cloud rat, here we go singing this song as if everyone was singing a version of this song, as if this song was part of a chorus of songs coming from the rafters and everyone we've ever known was joining in.

What we are made from Llin Island cloud rat is difficult to pin down. What composes our heartbeats is mysteriously nowhere to be found. Cloud rat there is comfort in knowing that what I am is just as nowhere to be found as what you were.

Llin Island cloud rat how does it feel to live from that place where there is no distinction between the function of my liver and the beating of your heart?

Between your thin layer of skin cloud rat, and my thin layer of skin, there is some space.

This space between us is simple. It is always weaving a pattern with itself. It is tangled up in all the illusions of separateness. It is driving around in automobiles. It is generous and makes no distinction between courage and fear.

Its job is to weave us all together. It is not confusing to the mind.

In between those two skins, that space is no more full of substance than inside our bodies covered in skin.

How does it feel to live from that place, from that no more full place of in between our very thin layers of skin?

Yunnan Box Turtle

Cuora yunnanensis

Turtle your carapace light to dark brown with three longitudinal ridges, turtle my red house with some blossoming fruit trees, my house amid the vineyards with the sulpher spray and the water table dropping, turtle your dark-brown head with a fine yellow line running from the nostrils to above the eye, ending in a neck stripe.

Turtle there is nowhere to blast off to. We are all imprisoned wherever we find ourselves right now. There is nowhere to stay in the shallow parts where maybe we can protect our fancy shoes. Turtle your throat and neck covered in yellow or orange marks, turtle my body recognizing itself as an illusion, my body with coffee and bread in it, my body creating a reality for itself to move around in.

Turtle of 2,000 meters high on the Yunnan Plateau in China, turtle of the high elevation wetland, turtle I am of the ridgeline above the fog line. I am of eight different homes in eight different years.

Turtle your habitat has been destroyed by the expanding city of Kunming. Turtle likely eaten out of existence due the demand of the Chinese food markets.

Turtle rich nations are responsible for greenhouse gases fuelling global warming, your China said on Tuesday, urging them to cut emissions and deflecting questions about whether Beijing will accept limits. Turtle your China hurtling towards possibly becoming the world's third-biggest economy by 2008, overtaking Germany and trailing only Japan and the United States, turtle most of that growth of your China fuelled by coal-burning power stations and wheezing factories.

Yunnan box turtle possibly affected by the fragmentation of China's large rivers caused by dams, turtle found in the Muséum national d'Histoire naturelle in Paris.

Turtle it is a miracle that anything exists at all and that amid all that exists turtle you no longer exist, and yet also turtle what I assume you shall assume for every atom belonging to me as good belongs to you.

Vegas Valley Leopard Frog

Lithobates fisheri

Before all the thoughts that became Fremont Street and the thoughts that became lots of slot machines and 3.99 all you can eat breakfast buffets, before anyone thought of a New York, New York casino with its roller coaster and its light pollution broadcasting across the sand all the way to Death Valley, before thoughts of sprawling, green slabs of lawn and the thought that watering these lawns is an important thing to do,

before the city and before the long journey that all the beings made to arrive at the city, before the wagons and the drying strips of meat, before the parched throats and cracked feet,

before the grasses in the lawns, before the disappearing aquifers and rivers, before the shifting jet streams and ocean currents and the depletion of deep, underground pockets

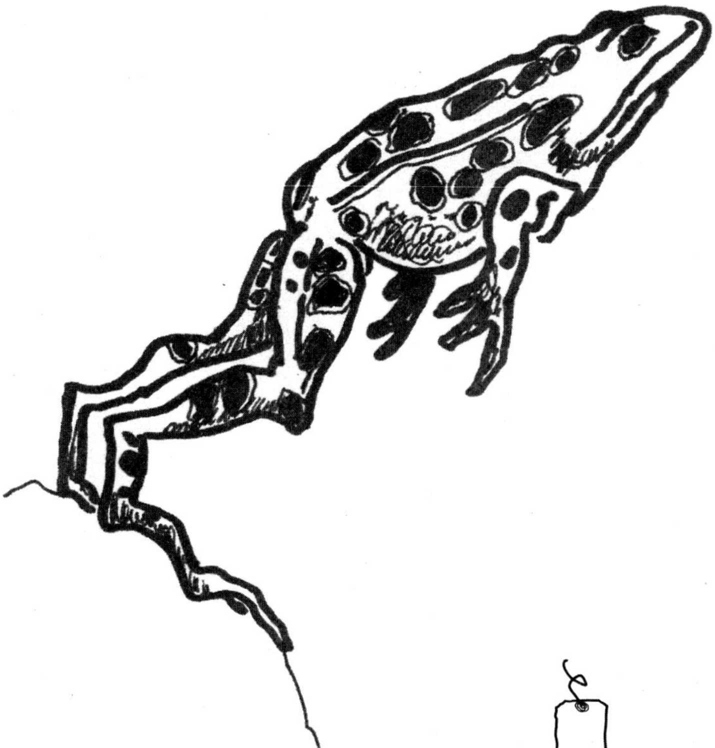

of oil, before even myself sitting here now far from Las Vegas on a cushion in the living room at war with myself, and at war with being at war with myself, before even these subtle wars within that I breathe into and sit patiently with,

the Vegas Valley leopard frog swam in the artisan springs of the Las Vegas Valley, frog who was two to three inches from nose to rear, who was olive green above with honey yellow hind limbs, who had pale stripes on the folds between his back and sides, whose legs were short and stocky, frog who lived in the artisan springs of the valley, whose waters formed a creek that flowed through the valley, forming an oasis in the desert, in the riparian corridors where there were willows and tules and cottonwoods.

The waters of these springs were captured and pumped to quench the growing city of Las Vegas, and the springs stopped flowing altogether by 1962, and now the Vegas Valley leopard frog is extinct evidently due to habitat loss resulting from spring capture and ground water pumping by the growing city of Las Vegas, and exacerbated by the introduction of the bullfrog.

This is not meant to be a fable going backwards, as if back there was a better place to be and there was a lesson back there, where there were more cottonwood trees, better than right here where there are more people. Everything since then has happened the way that it has happened because the leopard frog and the dried out springs happened the way that they did.

Even myself sitting here now, far from Las Vegas on a cushion in the living room, at war with myself and at war with being at war with myself, even these subtle wars within that I breathe into and sit patiently with.

Lesser Bilby
or Rabbit-Eared Bandicoot

Macrotis lecura

Lesser Bilby you were a marsupial the size of a young rabbit in the deserts of Central Australia. You preyed on rodents and were vicious, making savage, snapping bites, and harsh, hissing sounds toward any one trying to handle you. Bilby you were grey-brown fading to pale grey underneath with a white tail, known only from the Gibson and Great Sandy Deserts of arid Central Australia.

Bilby to truly sing this song that we are singing, this off pitch song that is exquisite in its non-perfection, this off pitch song that is coming from the rafters, that is coming from the bedrock, that is coming from the deserts and the swamps and the jungles and streams, the song that is the story of you, that is the story of our selves, that is the story of everybody else, to sing it clearly and not through cloudy shrouds of suffering.

Bilby you made burrows in the dunes two to three meters deep, and came out only at night.

Bilby, you were hunted out by foxes and feral cats. Bilby you could not compete with the cattle who were introduced to your continent, who grazed and grazed on the same grasses as you, who were bigger and hungrier and more useful to my species than you.

Bilby the latest record of you was a skull found in a wedge-tailed eagle's nest in 1967.

Bilby you are gone from the world, and here I am sitting in a chair in a cafe of the world, twirling around and around in this moment on the world. I am singing this off pitch song as if everyone was singing a version of the song, as if all the passengers on the spinning miracle boat were singing a version it, as if your passing was more than a dimple in the blanket that we stretch out and call time.

Western Black Rhinoceros

Diceros bicornis longipes

Sweet rhino the IUCN declared you tentatively extinct in 2006 and yet there are people who are convinced that you are not extinct, that you are, in small numbers, living secretively in the wild spaces of Northern Cameroon, you who labored gracefully under two glorious horns, you who grasped stems and branches and twigs and leaves from the trees with your upper lip.

Rhino a trio of experts systematically scoured 2,500 kilometers of habitat in Northern Cameroon last year, and this intensive survey failed to locate any sign of you, and still there are some people who are praying for you, rhino, and I am one of them.

You sweet and monstrous beast, you poached to the brink for your two fearsome horns, you rhino of West Africa who weighed up to 3,000 pounds.

Two horned rhino with your relatively pointed snout, with your pointed, prehensile lip, I am only just learning how to pray, how to hold space in a prayer for everything that is and was and will be true, how to hold not just what I want to be true in that prayer but to hold the poachers and the politics of the world in the prayer,

to hold the image of you lying in the dirt with a bloody gaping hole where the horns were rhino, without the thought of bad image good image, bad people good people in the prayer, to find the very subtle space where the prayer goes out, the space that is a silent, ringing space, the space that moves the prayers (that live most precisely in the nerves of my own arms and torso and legs) to the other side of the world, into the tall grasses of Cameroon, sweet rhino, where you may or may not still be living secretively in small numbers, grasping for the twigs with your pointed, prehensile lip.

Lake Victorian Cichlids

Paralabidochromis

There are so many places to get caught, everyday places like in the car that is covered in dust, or in a field full of very blue hills, a field that feels like it is much too beautiful to get caught in. Fish get caught in nets, moths get caught in light, I get caught in different jobs, in different circles of people. I get caught in loops, the same loops that my family has always been looping, until the fraying of any given loop takes the place of a circular movement around and around. I have been caught fascinated by what is being frayed and that place is as beautiful as the field full of very blue hills. Crane flies get caught in the house, crane flies who only have a few days to be alive, only a few days to do what they came here to do, to find who they came here to find. I find crane flies dead on the windowsills. I find them weak from banging into windowpanes. Cows get caught in barbed wire. A big snake got caught in the plastic webbing around the garden and with scissors I helped it to get free.

Lake Victoria lies in the Great Rift Valley in Tanzania, Uganda, and Kenya. Lake Victoria has a shoreline of 2,138 miles and has more than 3,000 islands, many of which have people living on them. The cichlids of Lake Victoria are a polygamous fish that grows to 15 centimeters in length. During spawning the males will take on much brighter colors. When it is time, the female picks up the eggs in her mouth and puts the lips of her mouth on the anal fin of the male who then ejaculates near her mouth to fertilize the eggs.

I am caught in a few yards of skin. It is dark inside the skin but somehow I am not caught in that darkness. I am caught in my five foot seven and in my 137 pounds. I am caught in my eye color and skin color and astrological chart. I am caught in this language and in these limited abilities of this body and this mind and this family and this country that I was born into. I love that I am caught in all these different ways. Within the confines of it there is more room than outside the confines of it. Within the confines of it there is a blooming that could never bloom outside the confines of it. Being caught is being held. It is a prison. It is one more way of getting free.

In Lake Victoria hundreds of species of the cichlids that lived there have gone extinct following the introduction of the Nile perch that was originally introduced for food. When the perch population exploded many of the cichlids were wiped out. Then people moved close to the lake to fish the perch. Then people chopped down trees for wood to burn in the kilns they use to dry the oily perch flesh. The trees hold the soil in place and when they were removed the waters became muddy. This new muddiness blinded the remaining cichlids and all the multitudes of species of cichlids became only a few species, because in all the mud they can't see their partners clearly enough to tell who is who and from what species.

Vultures are caught in ugly bodies with big, black wings. I am caught in a body without wings. Trees get caught as trees and spend hundreds of years slowly and patiently being as a tree. Gophers are caught digging holes in the ground. Cichlids are caught in Lake Victoria with the Nile perch eating everything there is to eat and the waters getting murkier and murkier. We are caught as patches of awareness amidst trillions and trillions of patches of awareness, and those just the patches of awareness that we have named. We are caught in these lives so full of grace, in these ancestral loops that must be good for us to be looping around because they are the only loops we have to work with. They are the only loops we could ever learn to get off of.

Hawaii ʻAkialoa

Hemignathus obscurus [obscurus]

The body is like a car that we drive in for awhile and then slowly the car begins to break down more and more, and especially if we live in a snowy place, the parts that used to be shiny on the car begin to gather rust and crud from the roads that connect our houses to other houses and to supermarkets and towns.

Inside of the body is hard to define, inside the muscles of the body, inside the left ventricles of the heart, inside the cartilage, the intestinal wall, is hard to define what is actually happening there, not the functions of the organs themselves but inside the function and beneath the function.

Inside the body that is alive everything is constantly dying. All the cells from all the organs constantly shedding and dropping off and being excreted or spit out through the mouth or sweat out through the armpit. Everything going away and going away, and then being replaced and then being replaced.

Before our bodies break all the way down we spend our whole lives breaking down, and breaking down other bodies in order to replenish the breaking down of our own bodies, which when broken and buried or burned become replenishment for other bodies still caught in this endless process of breaking and breaking down.

Yours is one heartbeat among trillions and trillions of heartbeats and these trillions and trillions of heartbeats are just the heartbeats that we can hear.

'Akialoa 'Akialoa 'Akialoa

'Akialoa you gathered nectar in a body that was tiny, that was as heavy as a teaspoon, that had a long beak and eyes that darted back and forth.

'Akialoa while you probed for nectar we were inventing the cell phone and the hybrid car. We were inventing the BlackBerry, the ipod, the vaccine for polio, artificial human limbs, contact lenses, a dependence on fossil fuels, the idea of fair trade, we were inventing clothing made out of hemp and kayaks made out of old bottles, and pogo sticks and legos and asphalt and pleather. We were inventing the World Wide Web and genetically modified corn. We were inventing smart bombs and the concept of wilderness while you probed for insects and nectar from flowers as big as my face, in the swamp called Alakai on the island of Kauai, away from the eyes of the inventions of the world.

Inside of your body 'Akialoa is hard to define, inside the wings fluttering and the feathers full of open space and the heartbeat that was beating while our heartbeats were beating while we were inventing while you hovered taking nectar from flowers as big as my face.

'Akialoa slowly the habitat of your swamp was made different by us. We took parts of it away and we introduced other parts from other places and the swamp became like a tightrope walker who lost her footing on an impossibly tenuous bit of hanging wire.

'Akialoa everything is constantly going away and going away and then being replaced and then being replaced.

'Akialoa you disappeared slowly and away from the eyes of the inventions and away from the eyes of the world, your wings beating, your small body hovering over flowers as big as my face in the swamp called Alakai on the island of Kauai, taking insects and nectar with your long beak.

Reminding us to compete yes, but to compete within limits, reminding us to not extinguish each other, to take only what we need from each other, reminding us to pollinate each other, to spread the seeds of each other far and wide to each other, to pass the nutrients from each to each other, reminding us to build sturdy structures in and around each other that lift smaller species up to the light of each other.

Meg Hamill is the author of the acclaimed book of poems, Death Notices. She currently lives in Sebastopol, California, where she works as an writer, and teaches with California Poets in the Schools. Read more, buy books, and e-mail Meg at www.meghamill.com.

Ted Keller is an active painter and teacher. He works in watercolor and lives, shows, and sells in Maine, (and soon, New Mexico). He currently teaches art classes at the University of Maine at Augusta. His work can be seen at tedkellerwatercolors.com and he can be contacted at tkeller@tidewater.net

Meg Hamill